TABLE OF CONTENTS

CHAPTER 11
Conclusion

CHAPTER ONE

A DAY OF INFAMY

At the age of 91, I have stories that are impossible for me to forget. Through the years I have tried time and again to erase them from my thoughts, but try as I may these occurrences keep coming back like a bad dream. There isn't a day that goes by when I don't think of that "Day of Infamy" as our President so aptly named it: December 7, 1941.

One may wonder how—after an interesting life, marriage, four children (all college educated), being in business, traveling and, above all, having a loving, understanding wife—these horrible memories won't fade. But they don't, and sometimes in the middle of the night I awake with a start and there they are, those dreadful occurrences that never leave me. So please indulge an old sailor and read on.

"THEY'RE JAPS! THEY'RE JAPS! I've seen them in Shanghai!"

With these words shouted in terror and surprise, Chief Wilkie, an "Old Salt" of more than 25 years in the Navy, woke us up to the fact that we were under attack by the Japanese Imperial Forces. This would turn out to be the worst attack inflicted on any American fighting force in our history. In the course of two hours, the mightiest battleships of our country were totally destroyed.

I say "woke us" because at that moment, my shipmates and I were standing still, frozen, wondering who and what were flying overhead.

The planes seemed to glide by as they dropped their deadly torpedoes on our battleships, conveniently lined up, two by two, like ducks in a row.

CHAPTER TWO

A BIT OF MY BACKGROUND

I was born in Los Angeles, California in 1924, to Florencio and Francisca Limón. I was the last of eight children. My father had emigrated from México in 1918 because, after eight years of constant revolution, living in México had become very dangerous, especially if one was of European stock like my father—"white" is how he would have been described.

My parents gave me all the riches of the world when they arrived in Los Angeles and made it possible for me to be born an American. My parents gave me the greatest legacy any parent can give an offspring. I do not say this lightly as being an American, to me, is the essence of who I am.

My mother died when I was two years old from the many complications of childbirth and a lack of medical care that we now take for granted. I never missed my mother, as I never knew her—in that way, nature was kind to me.

My father was my everything. Even though he was a strict disciplinarian, he taught me manners and characteristics that have served me well to this very day. One characteristic is having the ability to follow an order without deviation. That served me well in the Navy, and also throughout my life.

In the early 1930s, during the Great Depression, my father found himself unemployed. He was a writer for the Long Beach Symphony Orchestra, which had disbanded due to lack of funding. He had no choice; he had to "farm" us out to other families. Much to my good fortune, my older brother and I were sent to live with what we termed "Americans" or "Anglos."

Again good fortune was with me, as we went to live with a family named Broughton. Being born in Los Angeles of Mexican parents I was bilingual, which made it a lot easier to adjust to a new and strange household.

How well I recall the hot, nutritious food served three times a day. I say this because for families during the Depression, eating three times a day had become rarity. One of the fondest memories I have of the time we spent with Mrs. Broughton was that she always insisted upon us going to Sunday school, where we were taught manners, cleanliness and good behavior; afterward, were rewarded by the most delicious afternoon dinners I had ever experienced. After singing, "Yes, Jesus loves me, Yes Jesus loves me… the Bible tells me so!" we sat down to the best meatloaf and mashed potatoes one could wish for.

For some reason or another, probably Mrs. Broughton not being paid by my father or the county, my brother and I were sent to live with a Mrs. Mathews. There the atmosphere was cold and very structured. This was not a good place for a lonely kid. My older eight-year-old brother was equally as perplexed as I was by the move.

From this household I was sent alone to a certain Mrs. Herald. Her husband did not like me primarily because I was alive, and he constantly verbally abused me. On occasion he would pull my ears or bat me on the head for the slightest infraction of the rules, whatever the rules were. Still I have to say I was very lucky as all these homes were typical American homes—clean, good neighborhoods, nice shrubbery and lawns and even sidewalks. In the neighborhood where I was from, none of these things existed.

Most important, where we lived, the language was English. I learned that English was my language to use and understand. So when I enlisted in the Navy I was not among strangers. Yes, I was lucky indeed!

When I was 15, my father died. A part of me died with him, as my love and respect for him was so all encompassing.

By 1939, one of my older sisters was married and I went to live with her and her husband. At that point, I was counting the days until I could enlist in the Navy. Those were the slowest two years of my life.

CHAPTER THREE

THE NAVY

Two months after I became 17, I went to downtown L.A. to the Naval Recruiting Office. In this immaculate office I was greeted by a Chief Petty Officer with more stripes than a zebra. He politely inquired why I wanted to enlist. I found out later that this was "form"—something they asked every guy who walked into their office. The message was that the Navy didn't need you. It was up to you to want to be in the Navy and to have the drive to become a good sailor.

Because of my age, I had to have a court-appointed legal guardian act as my "father." The man signed papers granting me permission to join the U.S. Navy. As soon as he signed my papers he left. I never heard from him again.

Evidently I met the Navy's requirements as they sent me to the Naval Training Station in San Diego, California, where I entered training in March of 1941. I trained for three months; it was very rigid and obedience to orders was first and foremost. Here is where my father's training paid off. I had no problem marching, reading, cleaning and standing watch at odd hours without complaining. I did exactly what the Navy wanted from its men, what was necessary in order to create good sailors.

After completing training, I was offered a choice of schools I could attend. One was aviation radio, for which I immediately applied. It was my first choice because I was going to get the chance to fly! At the time that would be the culmination of my dreams, the opportunity to fly —and fly with the Navy! The other reason I chose aviation radio was because I had to pass a code test, which to me was really more of a musical test. I passed with flying colors. I never had a doubt because I have always been "in tune" with music.

I loved music. My father played clarinet and saxophone ("the reeds" is what he called them) and upright bass. He was first chair in the orchestra—that meant he was good, but at the time I was too young to understand what it meant to be the first char. I do remember being impressed that he wore a tuxedo. So passing what seemed like a fairly straightforward musical test was no problem for me.

In the Navy, if you could type you were accepted as a trainee for radio because when the messages came in, they came in rapidly and you had to type them on a standard typewriter keyboard. I could type 60 words per minute, which in those days that was a big deal. The typewriters weren't like they are today. The keys were heavy and you had to push them down hard. I remember pounding on that keyboard until my fingers were sore.

After completing my Naval training in San Diego, I was ready to enter Aviation Radio School. Like most young men at the time I wanted to be a pilot or fly as a crewmember aboard any Naval aircraft. It could be the highest accomplishment of my young life, to fly as an American in the best navy in the world.

CHAPTER FOUR

RACISM-I LEARN TO FIGHT BACK

As excited and proud as I was to have been accepted into the Navy, there was one facet that I would face and to this day continue to not understand—racism of the worst kind. I remember a blond recruit from Texas who did not hesitate to say to me, "You're Mexican? You know in Texas we consider Mexicans just like we do niggers!"

I had not learned how to verbally counter racism at that time so I resorted to the only answer I knew, fighting back physically. Some of these bigoted recruits were men in their late 20s and early 30s. They were fully developed men and I was a slight, 155-pound, 17-year-old boy. I had to think twice about accepting any challenge, even though this was a very direct challenge to my manhood and background. Several times I was completely humiliated, but I only fumed and wished, "If my older brothers were here, they would show these bigots where to go!"

My humiliation was made worse because in my family my father had been white. He was often addressed in English and the person addressing him would be totally perplexed when my father could only answer him in Spanish. At the time people thought that if you were white you certainly must speak English. Anglos could not understand that white people could be something other than Americans. In fact, my older brothers were always thought of as Americans, as they were white and spoke English as all Americans did. How I wished they were there to protect me against these biased and bigoted recruits.

So it happened during training that one of them, named Lewis, finally went too far and I had to fight back. I will be polite and use a censored version of what he said, "Hey Mex, you shouldn't even be in the Navy and be in the company of white men. Your mother should have aborted you!"

Yep—he'd gone too far and I had to fight. The fight began, and he came at me in a ferocious rush and I thought surely this would be the end of me. I hit him with an uppercut, followed by a right punch. This stopped him for the moment and we started to circle each other. Of course by now everybody in the barracks was taking one side or the other. There were good guys on my side, my buddies. On his side were the bad guys, the bigots. My buddies were shouting, "Get him Limón, punch him again!" The bigots were shouting, "Kill the Mex!"

Right there in my fear and desperation I learned that I could fight. I started to move, jab, cross him with a right to his jaw. I was far swifter and could move much faster than my opponent. He staggered as I hit him with a hard right. Now I smelled blood as he staggered again. I kept hitting his jaw with all my might and all the hate that was in me. Finally, he staggered towards one of the bunks and he said, "I give up, I give up!"

My guys hollered and shouted in my favor. Lewis was totally bloodied with his eyes swollen shut. He sat down on the bunk, bruised and beaten.

Much later—it was during the second year of the war—on some forgotten island, my shipmates and I were working, repairing one of our aircraft by flashlight in the middle of the night. We were using flashlights so as not to attract a Japanese night attack. As we worked one of the sailors asked me, "Say isn't your name Limón?"

I answered that it was and he said, "I remember you in San Diego before the war when you beat up that tough guy Lewis. That was a hell of a fight!" I answered, "Thanks for remembering, how is Lewis?" His answer stunned and saddened me. He said, "Lewis was discharged before the war. You partially destroyed his eyesight."

I couldn't believe it. I certainly didn't mean to end Lewis' career in the Navy. I was simply fighting back, fighting for my dignity and my manhood. As I think of it all now, perhaps he went back to civilian life and led a good life and didn't get killed or wounded during the raid on Pearl. Maybe I did him a favor and he lives to this very day. I certainly hope so.

I later found out that racism was not limited to being against Mexicans or blacks. The old salts who had done duty in the American Asiatic Fleet were totally disdainful of the Japanese Imperial Navy. In bull sessions where the old salts prevailed, they said, "Those little yellow bastards could not fly, they had old fashioned aircraft, they could not see at night, their ponderous ships were clumsy." The topper was, "If they can't beat the Chinks, how the hell can they beat us?"

This racist attitude permeated every rank from the old salts to the Admirals and Generals in command—especially those charged with the defense of the Hawaiian Islands. It took only two hours for those "little yellow bastards" that couldn't fly to lay waste to our fleet and our American pride, and murder hundreds of our soldiers. And all with a precision that left us amazed and astounded.

But racism continued; we could not face the fact that the Japanese were experts at the art of war and surprise attack. Immediately the rumor began that the Germans had planned it all—there was this idea that only the white German mind could be capable of planning and conducting such a clever and complete victory. As the war continued, this rumor died. We began to recognize that the Japanese were experts at war.

Years later, as I read the Japanese war books I learned that the Japanese, in turn, were racist to the point of disdain for us as fighting men.

CHAPTER FIVE

ONE UNWISE CHOICE CHANGES MY LIFE

After graduation from Aviation School we were all given our preference as to where we would like to be stationed. The choices were: go to Panama or Corpus Christi, Texas, stay in San Diego or go to Hawaii. Of course I jumped at the chance to go to Hawaii simply because of the lure and the beauty of the islands, not to mention the many movies made by Bing Crosby and Bob Hope. The movies depicted Hawaii as a beautiful and fun place with girls, music and romance. The chance to go to Hawaii for a kid from East L.A. was truly a big deal and an adventure far beyond anything I could have imagined at the time. Little did I know that I was walking into a very dark chapter of history.

In October of 1941, I became a crewmember of the USS Swan, an aircraft tender. The Swan's mission was to refuel, repair and afford lodging for aircrews while away from the main bases. The theory was that seaplanes could operate hundreds of miles toward enemy territory. These amphibian aircraft could cover seas in advance of our main forces, then fly home to the mother ship and be made ready for the following flights. This was a great theory, but in effect one would always be out on the proverbial "banana peel." Theories had a way of playing out differently than expected in real life.

Before the war I found myself in Hawaii, ready to fly! But first I had to do a year of sea duty aboard a Naval vessel. That was the rule at the time. One year of sea duty; then, and only then, could one enter a Squadron and become an "Airdale," as we were known. As a crewmember aboard the USS Swan, I would fulfill my year of sea duty. I had to do my duties as a radioman aboard the ship. As radiomen, we stood watch for four hours on, and eight hours off. We copied any and all messages on the main circuit known as "FOX." All messages emanating from the central command, Pearl Harbor, were known as "CINCUS" which stood for "Commander-in-Chief, US" Fleet. This was also known, in radio terms, as "F5L" based at Pearl Harbor.

<u>As a "Striker" Aboard Ship</u>

Now, when you copy code, you don't dare make a mistake in the copying of that message. So you sit there with one of the experienced radiomen and you copy as he copies until the chief determines that you are a capable radioman. By copy, I mean, somebody sends a message and you copy it as you would a phone call, only it's in code. For example he's saying NIJP (that's the USS Swan) from F5L (that would be commander in chief, US Fleet, Pearl Harbor). If he has anything to say to you, for whatever reason, he uses NIJP, the radio call sign for the USS Swan. While you copy everything that comes over the circuit, it's all in code. The code is all numbers and letters and, as radiomen, we did not even know the context of the message. The message could be QURTZ followed by five numbers. The only people who knew the context were the decoding officers. The only thing we knew was the heading. For example, if it were for us, NIJP, we would take it up to the bridge, to the captain and the decoding officer.

F5L, being commander-in-chief of the US Fleet, was in total control of the circuit. He would send out messages to a ship, carrier, or battleship with whom he needed to communicate. He would code the messages according to urgency. "Zero" might mean urgent. The strict rule was that no one was to transmit out of order. If we wanted to transmit a message we'd have to ask for permission of F5L. It was all very orderly. I relay this here because it was this very system that broke down the day of the attack.

CHAPTER SIX

I BECAME CLOSE TO THE BLACK STEWARDS

As I have mentioned before, the Navy was racist. I knew it, being a Mexican-American boy, but it didn't make any difference to me because I was very proud to be in the Navy. I was excited to go to radio school and that I was going to fly as a radioman. I first went on the ship to do my year of sea duty. Our captain was Lt. Commander John Leslie Hall, Jr., an Annapolis graduate, and a real gentleman. I got to know him as I handed him messages. I had to go up to the bridge and hand him the message board. He would sign, keep his copy, and I would thank him and step aside.

As I delivered messages to the captain on the bridge, the captain and the other officers were using words and terminology I could not understand. For example, I overheard one of the officers say, "We were not given the latitude to carry out this program."

I was confused, as in high school the word "latitude" was always used together with longitude, in other words, in geographical terms. I had no idea that the word "latitude" could be used in any other way.

The more I went to the bridge, the more curious I became as to the use of language. It finally occurred to me that I must acquire a dictionary in order to understand what these highly trained, Annapolis graduates were saying and meaning. I recall another phrase that completely astounded me, which was "...the avidity of the crew in search of their sexual desires while on leave!"

There were many more new words I started to hear and came to understand, which increased my love for the English language.

Anyway, there were two stewards, black sailors, whose sole job was to take care of the officers (the captain, the engineering officer, executive officer, etc.). These stewards did the officers' laundry and cooking and they served the officers with silver place settings. I'd never seen silver in my life. They used linen and the stateroom where the officers ate was elegant.

Well, I got to know the stewards, Quinn, who was a big guy, and Lawless who was my weight. At that time, everybody wanted to be Joe Lewis, the great champion. Now that I knew I could fight, we would box all the time on the gun deck, anytime we had some time off. Lawless and I would start sparring and then Quinn and I would box. Quinn would treat me like a little brother. We didn't have headgear and Quinn, who was a big guy, would spar with me and pat me on the head, and he'd call me "Leeee-mone." He couldn't say "Limon." Both he and Lawless were from the South. Everything had the emphasis on the wrong syllable.

So we'd work out, and I got to be their friend. Whenever they cooked and had anything left in the way of goodies, pies, cakes, which they always did, Quinn would come by afterwards and ask, "Leeee-mone, you want some of this?"

Because the captain was from the South, they used to have corn fritters, often with honey on them. Quite a treat!

I'd say, "Hey, Quinn, I'll take it!"

Sometimes Quinn would hand me a tremendous roast with all the fixings. As he went by the radio shack he would offer me the leftover food from the captain's table. He would hand it to me, and I would put it in the safe with a combination lock. Quinn and Lawless wouldn't give this food to anybody else but me. I always wondered what those other radiomen thought about getting the goodies that I shared with them.

The only reason they were getting them was because of my friendship with Quinn and Lawless.

The officers had excellent cooks in Quinn and Lawless. The officers' mess had its supply of food, they never got any of their food from the crew's supplies. They bought their own, so of course they bought the best, and Honolulu had the best. All in all, I was living in clover.

Another way I shared friendship with Quinn and Lawless was through music. I had brought some records with me from the states from that great show by Duke Ellington, "Jump for Joy," with all that wonderful music like "Take the A Train." Herb Jeffries was on the record singing, "Flamingo." Ivie Anderson sang, "I Got it Bad, and That Ain't Good." There was a comedian "Wonderful Smith"—it was a great show. The ship had a little portable record player and we'd wind it up and play the music. Sadly enough, there was a group of guys, especially the deck force, who didn't like this "nigger" music. Please pardon the expression, it was theirs. They didn't like the way we were getting along so well. In those days the black people didn't talk to the white people—not on our ship, anyway.

A Heartbreaking Story

One day as we finished our workout, Lawless and I sat down and he told me about his experience, which I found heartbreaking: "Pete, you don't realize how difficult it is to grow up as a black man. Where I'm from," he was from the deep South, "you have to step off the sidewalk if a white person is coming towards you. You don't dare look a white woman in the eye because people may holler 'rape!' You can't do what we are doing now!" In the South, at that time, Lawless and I could never have worked out together, much less sat down and had a conversation. I'd say Lawless was 19 or 20. He pointed out that things were not entirely different on the ship: "Man, you're not allowed to be a man on ship, we don't even have a gun position."

Blacks weren't allowed to go near the weapons. Years later it occurred to me why it was that way. Historically, the powerful elite in America never wanted to arm the black people thinking they might get "out of line." Lawless told me how he had enlisted in the Navy because he didn't have any choice. He wanted to see the world, and also after 20 years he'd have a pension. In those days we were all geared for that. You get in the Navy, you do your 20 years, you'd be only 37, 38 and you'd have a pension. He said, "There isn't anything out there for black men. You work for nothing. You work in factories 10 hours a day, six days a week."

He told me about the oppression that black men had to endure to just make a living. Lawless was forlorn as he told me this story. I was quiet as I could be. I knew some of it, being Mexican-American, but I personally had never experienced any of this. I knew some people who had, however. When Lawless sat there looking at me, I understood he would never tell anybody else but me that story. In a sense I was honored that he had the confidence in me. All I could say to him was "I know, I know, I'm sorry." What else could I say? I didn't know what to say. To this day, I still think to myself, what do you tell a guy who tells you he is stripped of his manhood simply because he's not white? Lawless and I stayed good friends and kept in touch for decades. In 1996, I wrote a letter to *U.S. News and World Report* magazine. They published it:

Military Injustice: "Military Injustice" [Cover, May 6] brought back a relevant, moving memory. While attending the 50th anniversary of Pearl Harbor, we were fortunate to be addressed by that brilliant black man, Gen. Colin Powell, then chairman of the Joint Chiefs. This address took place at the Pearl Harbor naval yard, within walking distance of where, 50 years before, our ship, the USS Swan, was dry-docked during the attack. As we listened to General Powell, my mind kept wandering to two of my shipmates who were not allowed to have a battle station simply because they were black! These two sailors were "stewards"—their only job was to cater to commissioned officers. I had developed a close relationship with both, as I was the only crewman willing and able to box with them. One day, after a workout, one of them movingly explained and complained as to the unfairness of life as a black man. As a boy of 17, I could only listen and feel sorry; I had no answers. As General Powell congratulated us and wished us well, I could only think of the two men and strongly wished that they had been there so that they could see that 50 years later, our top military man was black! By the way, during the attack, the two "passed the ammunition" along with the rest of us. I don't think anyone would have had the temerity or the stupidity to prevent them from being fighting men that day!

Peter T. Limon
San Clemente, Calif.

On the day Pearl Harbor was attacked, Quinn and Lawless became fighting men. They, along with everybody else, had access to the ammunition. But to my regret at the 50th anniversary, as I looked around at the convention center in Honolulu, even though I asked everybody if anybody knew Quinn or Lawless, unfortunately nobody did.

CHAPTER SEVEN

THE ATTACK

Ordinarily, on Sunday mornings soldiers and sailors went to church. You could go to Mass, to Temple, to the Protestant church. After church, it was a day of rest and we would go ashore to Honolulu. We would play ball, go to the beach, and in the evenings go to the clubs.

The Japanese philosophy of war (we read this later) is to "attack the enemy on the snowiest night of the year, at three in the morning." This means, of course, look for a vulnerable part of the military schedule. The Japanese knew that Sunday morning was when we were vulnerable.

We had never been attacked in this fashion before; therefore we had no reason not to carry on as usual. It was an open secret that our military had the day off on Sunday. That the Japanese chose to attack us that morning, December 7th, a Sunday, should not have been a total surprise.

We were just having a good time. I called it the "Country Club Navy", and the "Country Club Army", because having a good time in Hawaii at the time (before the war that is) was why you went there. We were always ashore having a good time.

That's me, on the very right

Of course we always did our duty as sailors, but nobody was serious about defending the harbor. Oddly enough, we were ready when we would leave the harbor. We were at "battle ready," everybody was at battle stations, but that's only when we were leaving the harbor. When we were tied up in the harbor we were not at our gun positions.

The morning of the attack on Pearl Harbor, we were in dry-dock, and I was going up for the 8-12 watch (eight in the morning until noontime). I'd become a radioman, and I was very proud of that. I thought, "My goodness, for a kid out of East Los Angeles, I'm now standing watch and at the age of 17!"

I was about to go up to the radio shack when I noticed an airplane gliding right past us. I could have hit him with the apple I was eating. I remember thinking that they were funny-looking airplanes. The machine gunner in the rear seat looked like an Eskimo with a fur-lined helmet. He turned around and pointed his machine-gun at us—Chief

Wilkie and me. Standing near me was also a young man whose name I don't recall, a thin young man. We looked at the first plane, then the second one, then the third one and that's when they started dropping torpedoes right up against the battleships.

Pearl Harbor is a very small harbor. At that point Chief Wilkie hollered, "THEY'RE JAPS! I've seen 'em before in Shang-hai!"

The kid said, "JAPS?! I didn't even know the Japanese were mad at us!"

Well, I had to chuckle, because under the conditions, it was a classic remark. So I ran up the ladder to get to my gun position, which was right next to the radio shack. As I went by the radio shack, I saw Michaels (one of the top radiomen in the business), who had panicked and thrown his headset against the typewriter, and hollered, "Somebody take over this fucking circuit!" Guns had begun to fire throughout the harbor but being in the small, confined radio shack, Michaels didn't know what was going on.

I ran in because it was my watch—it was eight in the morning. I took over the circuit and I started to copy the most unusual messages ever heard over a Naval radio circuit. It said, "090" (that meant all ships at sea, from F5L). "Pearl under attack by Japanese naval units. THIS IS NO DRILL! THIS IS NO DRILL!"

Well then, at that point, everybody from all over the Pacific, every ship afloat, every base, started to request ZMA IMI, meaning, "Verify your last message." They could not believe what they were hearing. Well, we understood how they couldn't, because who would believe that Pearl Harbor was under attack?

So with that in mind I would copy the messages and send them up to the bridge vocally. At that point the chief came in and took over and I ran out to my gun position. It was a 1917 Louis-British machinegun. It looked like a stovepipe. Croft, the gunners mate, who ordinarily would have handled it very easily, couldn't find the keys to the ammunition locker. Well, it wasn't my job to have keys to the lockers, so I had to stand around while he was searching for them. Meanwhile, whoever could open fire in the harbor had opened fire. You can best describe it all as bedlam. Finally Croft somehow opened up the ammunition boxes and we loaded the machine gun and fired it, and in all, gunners-mate Croft fired three rounds... it sounded like "tek, tek, tek" and that was the end. It jammed and would not continue firing. This young man who was so efficient, ordinarily, started to cry and hit the machine gun saying, "This fucking machine gun won't work! IT WON'T WORK, IT WON'T WORK, IT WON'T WORK!"

I came to the conclusion if he couldn't make it work, I couldn't make it work, so I ran to help wherever else I could.

Meanwhile, we were all like Keystone Cops, going back and forth—to one side of the ship, and then the other. Then, a strong, clear and loud voice shouted: "GET THE GUNS GOING, GET THE GUNS GOING! Don't let these bastards do this to us!" That strong voice came from a second-class cook named Cox. He, and he alone, had assumed the mantle of leadership. You never know where leadership is going to come from. In effect, there was no leadership, until Cox commanded us to fight back. How odd that it took a cook.

So I got in line, and we started passing the boxes of ammunition. All of a sudden, somebody hollered, "Hey you bunch of assholes, you're sending up the wrong kind of ammunition." So somebody down below switched to the kind that fit the weapon.

That was the basis of the attack for me: we did what we could. We kept firing and we saw some airplanes being downed. But primarily the damage had already been done. It took a mere 10 or 15 minutes for the torpedo planes to lay waste to an entire fleet. By that time, all the battleships were on fire and burning, guys were jumping into the water and we were trying to get out of dry-dock to go help. The rest of the attack, by dive-bombers and fighter planes, lasted about two hours.

Eventually the captain came aboard. We slid out of dry-dock and went out to help wherever we could. We pulled away and tied up next to the Battleship California, which was off by itself. The Battleship Arizona had just been blown to pieces, and we didn't want to be near it or the rest of the battleships.

There are one or two newsreels on Pearl Harbor that show our ship spraying our hoses out at the battleships that remind me of little boys peeing on a bonfire. The fires and damage were far too large, our attempts to do anything to help far too small. I recalled that I had copied a message that stated that, "TRANSPORTS HAVE BEEN SIGHTED OFF BARBERS POINT!" This added to the horror of the day, "Now we are going to be invaded," I thought.

I remember thinking, now that our fleet is gone, the Japanese are going to land. That weighed heavily on my mind as I reported it to the bridge, because I had no idea we'd ever have to fight on land.

As it was, that evening after the raid we were all handed a rifle and 90 rounds of ammunition and a bayonet. The captain lined us all up and told us, "THE NAVY DOESN'T SURRENDER, we're going to fight for the harbor."

We believed that the Japanese were going to land. I thought at that moment, “I can’t believe I’ve gotten into all of this.” I thought I’d come to Honolulu to have a good time and become a radioman, learn something, and be happy. But here we were in this unimaginable fix. Then and now this is something that is very difficult to convey—the idea that you are going to be invaded and have to fight as infantrymen, bayonet to bayonet. My mind recoiled at the thought.

On the next page is a map of Pearl Harbor depicting how the ships were on the day of the attack.

I wanted to make sure the map filled an entire page so you can more clearly see the location of the ships. The Japanese planes flew in from off to the right center on the map, flying into the harbor where the ships sat like helpless sitting ducks.

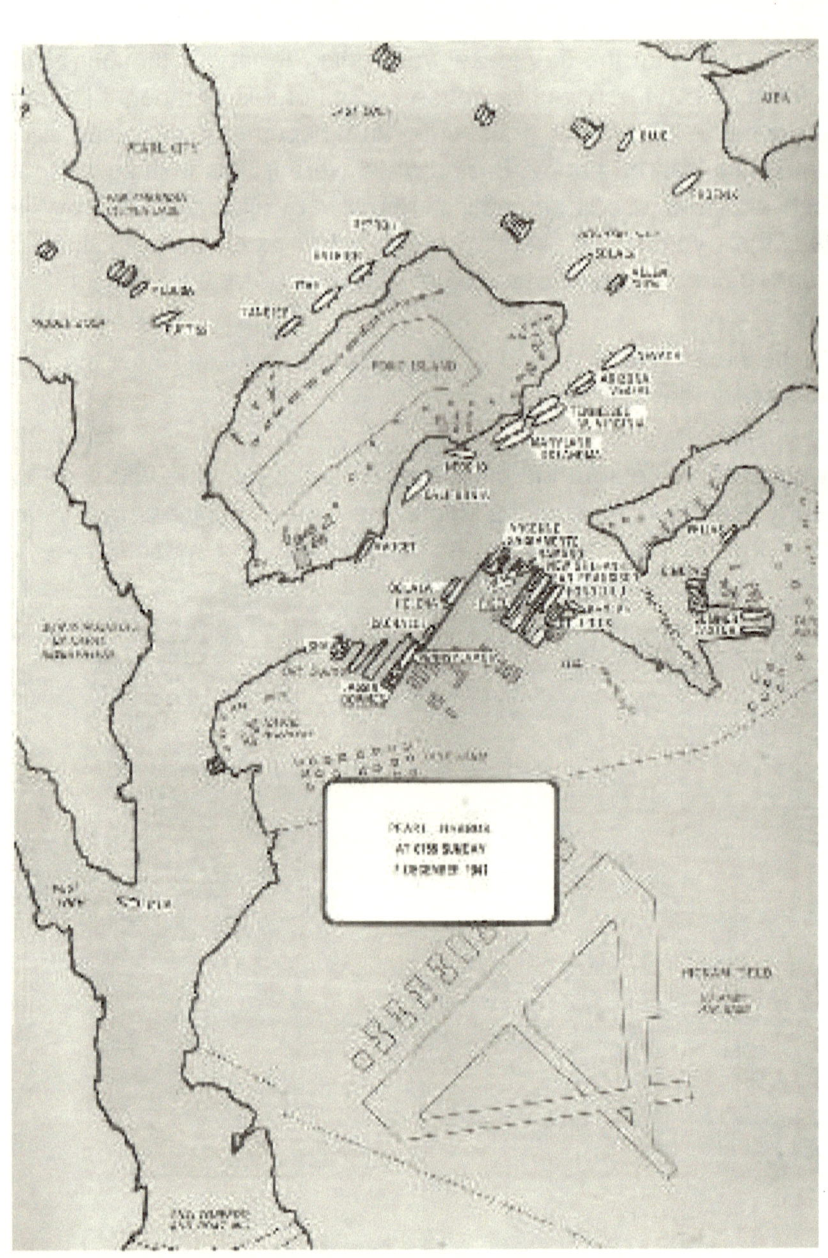
PEARL CITY
AIEA
FORD ISLAND
HICKAM FIELD
PEARL HARBOR

How did they get so close?

I remember that I didn't know how I felt. I knew I was angry to put it politely. I was befuddled and I think I can speak for many people in the harbor, or even on the Island as I wondered, "But how did they get so close? Why is it that we didn't know?"

The United States had been in what we thought was friendly communication with the Japanese. In hindsight, how we ever depended upon diplomacy is beyond me. It was commonly known in 1939 that modern war had changed. Surprise attacks had become the norm. The Germans had attacked the Poles without any warning, specifically in one of their harbors where a German battleship, allegedly visiting, docked right next to a fort and at a given signal they opened fire on the fort, destroying it completely. Then the Germans attacked the Russians with massive force, June 22, 1941, again without warning.

Another thing is, we knew (I knew because I'd always been a history reader) that in 1940 the British carriers attacked the Italian fleet in the harbor at Taranto and they caught them exactly the way the Japanese caught us—completely by surprise. The British carriers launched their ancient biplanes armed with torpedoes and sank most of the Italian fleet. The only difference is that they had been at war for a year. At least the British and the Italians knew that they were at war.

So if I, a 17-year-old kid, knew about the British attack (the similarities, that is, using aerial torpedoes to attack a harbor) I could only assume my superiors knew. Our Admirals must have known that we could be attacked by carrier close to the Island of Hawaii, in this case Oahu. They must have known that we would be completely defenseless on a

Sunday morning. They knew we all went to church and spent the rest of the day having a good time.

We knew that the harbor was good against a storm, but it wasn't good militarily, because it was narrow and overcrowded. The fleet was lined up perfectly for a torpedo attack. We thought the harbor was too shallow, torpedoes wouldn't work, whatever. But when you're an Admiral or a General, you study war. If I'd have been the Admiral there in Hawaii, I feel I would have been aware of the British attack on the Italian fleet in Taranto.

What many people don't even know is that nine years before the attack, in 1932, Pearl Harbor was attacked by carrier aircraft and was taken totally by surprise. Luckily, this time it was only a war maneuver by our own carriers that steamed out of San Diego, travelled the distance to Pearl Harbor and simulated a surprise attack. I can only conclude that nothing was learned by that maneuver. It's so easy to play Monday morning quarterback now, of course.

A Tragedy Of Major Proportions

On the night of the attack, it happened again, another tragedy of major proportions. We were all at our gun positions and the night was very dark. Of course it's always raining in Honolulu. Not only was it dark because it was nighttime, but also the smoke emitting from the battleships completely clouded the sky. We saw coming at us four airplanes with their landing lights on. We opened fire. I remember we started to shoot straight up, shooting at anything.

These planes were coming in to land at Ford Island. We were right next to the Battleship California, which was tied up to Ford Island. We were firing directly at these airplanes. We then saw fires as some of the airplanes went down. The next day we got the report—it turned out they were our own carrier airplanes.

The heartbreak continues to this day. Why would somebody send our own carrier planes into Pearl Harbor at night when all we could see were landing lights? We were now the biggest bunch of trigger-happy sailors and marines who were completely engrossed in shooting at anything and anybody that moved—and by accident, this included each other. No one has ever explained this and we may never know.

CHAPTER EIGHT

"DOC" RELATES THIS MOST UNUSUAL OF STORIES

This story is unusual because we have never read about it in print—not in newspapers, magazines or history books. Doc was our corpsman, someone similar to a medic who gives temporary relief before getting the wounded to a hospital. Every ship has a corpsman or two and when he returned, at least two weeks later, to the ship this was Doc's story.

Immediately after the attack on Pearl Harbor, Doc disappeared from the ship. Since there were only two men with light wounds on our ship to care for, he was called away to give much needed help at the nearby Naval hospital. We understood they were overwhelmed with wounded and pleading for help over the radio.

One can only imagine an emergency ward geared to take care of a normal number of emergencies now being asked to treat hundreds of critically wounded men in a matter of a few hours! They found themselves totally lacking in the number of trained personnel needed for such a horrible emergency. They pleaded for help from anyone with any medical experience, and from any volunteers willing to help. It was like a scene out of *Dante's Inferno*.

As he told us the story, you could see by the expression on his face that he was now a totally tortured man. His face was vacant with that far away stare, he was visibly in pain. He told us there were hundreds of wounded with so many types of wounds. Some, he said, were totally covered with oil to the point where you could not determine their wounds. He worked for days with not only doctors and nurses, but also with volunteers who clearly had never worked in a hospital.

As he assisted the medical people, he noticed several white women taking the wounded sailors into the showers in order to remove the black oil from their bodies so that the doctors could determine where they were wounded. By this time, Doc had learned that the women were prostitutes from Honolulu, doing all they could do to help. As he worked with one of the young white women, he became friendly and they talked during brief breaks. Doc said that during one of the breaks the pretty, redheaded young woman said to him, "I am not one of them" and she pointed at some of the other girls working with the staff. She related her story to him. "I am from Kansas. I came to Honolulu on a promise of work. I had read an article that there was a job opening for a secretary in Honolulu. They said it was for decent pay, and all transportation and expenses paid."

She said she could not imagine such an opportunity, as this was in the late 1930s and a job, no matter where, was a job! She arrived in San Diego where she met a kindly middle-aged woman. This woman helped her board the ship bound for Honolulu, second class. She said she was overjoyed and extremely happy to be headed to that "paradise" in the Pacific, to begin her career.

Once in Honolulu, she was greeted by a very well dressed man who said he was the manager of the company where she would be working. He drove her to "Hotel Street" where, unbeknownst to her, the houses of prostitution were. Once there, she was introduced to a woman who showed her to a room. This woman turned out to be the Madame of the house.

At the time, she thought it was odd that other women were walking around in shorts or kimonos—see-through kimonos. As she started to ask questions, the Madame curtly said to her, "Shut up and do as you're told!" She told the doc that she replied, "I'm getting the hell out of here!"

As she walked downstairs towards the exit door, she was stopped by a hulking Hawaiian pimp who shoved her and told her to go back upstairs. She tried to push him aside, but he was too big, too strong, and he slapped her across the face. She fell backwards onto the floor. As she got up, he hit her again and again, repeating in broken English, "You go upstairs, you go upstairs!"

In her desperation she cried out to one of the girls, "Please call the police, please call the police!" But the other girls met her calls with stony silence. They did not call the police, nor did they show any sympathy.

She staggered up to her room and washed the blood off her face. In her anger, she still demanded to be let out of that horrible place. But the Madame said to her, "You are here because you want to be, so relax and we will talk later!"

The girl from Kansas told Doc that soon after her first beating the pimp who had greeted her at the dock in Honolulu Harbor entered her room. She thought she could appeal to his good conscience, and she asked him to help her be released. But all he said to her was "Take off your clothes!"

She told him to go to hell. He called in the hulking Hawaiian pimp, and between the two, they tore her dress off and took turns raping her. She told Doc that finally, out of sheer exhaustion, "I succumbed."

That, she said, was the beginning of her life as a prostitute, tragically, and sadly.

While we don't know for sure what happened to this redheaded, freckle-faced girl from Kansas, Doc did go on to tell another side to this brave girl's story.

This girl knew all about weapons as she had grown up hunting with her father. She was familiar with the service automatic Colt .45, as her father had served in France during World War I and had kept a .45 when he came home. She was taught to fire it, field strip it, and she became a good shot. Because she was being brutalized into submission, she told Doc that she wished she'd had this weapon available and that she would not have hesitated to kill the white pimp and the burly Hawaiian pimp who had both raped her repeatedly.

While doing "tricks" before the war started, she met and liked a blonde boy from the Midwest who had a lot in common with her. This was a young sailor by the name of Broadman. She became close enough to ask him if he could somehow get a .45 for her. He said he would if he could get it off the ship, but it would not be easy because it was bulky. He told her that each time he left the ship he had to show whatever was in his shaving kit, and that a weapon would be difficult to hide.

She suggested that he disassemble the weapon to get it off the ship, part by part. Boardman thought this could work, but that it would take time. She said she could wait, as she needed the weapon badly for her protection from the characters running the whorehouse. She wanted to kill the two pimps. Doc said that this girl had been very serious about this as she told him the story.

Doc asked her how she happened to hear that help was needed at the hospital. She replied that the radio kept blaring that urgent help was needed. Anyone with medical skills—actually, anyone who would volunteer—was desperately needed. She left the whorehouse with the rest of the girls by pulling a knife on the Hawaiian pimp and telling him: "Step aside, you SOB, because next to being a whore, I am a patriot!"

She related that she surely would have used the knife on this pimp whom she hated with a passion. As she ran out, the rest of the girls followed and they drove to the hospital to help. To me this story is legendary. Perhaps these girls were short on luck, but not on patriotism.

As it was, she never got any weapon and Doc could only assume that she was evacuated to the mainland when the Navy gave any and all Americans the ability to go back to the states, as they would only be a liability if Hawaii were invaded. Doc told us that being evacuated back to the mainland is the way he thinks she finally got out of the horrible, sordid life she found herself in.

As I've continued to think about this abused young lady, I can't help but wonder how the people in power could live with this abomination happening right under their very noses. They had full knowledge of it! As we all know, corrupt conditions can only exist with the knowledge and approval of the people in power. This goes for the cop on the beat all the way up to the governor. At that time, the "territory of Hawaii" had a governor appointed by our very own country.

What is important about this story is the complete, unabashed patriotism shown by these women, with no thought of their personal safety; they helped —tending to the wounded servicemen after that horrible day. To me it's an extreme example of "patriotism" at its best, yet to my knowledge, no mention or recognition of their valorous acts has ever been given.

CHAPTER NINE

THE REASON FOR THE WAR: SEARING PREJUDICE ON BOTH SIDES

Japan and the United States had been on a collision course since 1905. The Japanese had just destroyed the whole Russian fleet in the Battle of Tsushima. Their fleet, modeled after the British fleet, was not only aggressive but also extremely confident.

Fighting and defeating a European power was very much in their militaristic thinking. Their minds were completely militaristic, in fact, in that they wanted to make their mark against the white world and claim their share of colonies as the European nations had done.

So in the early part of the twentieth century, they were driven toward conquest and acquisition of colonies with the needed materials for this island nation. But most of all, the Japanese considered themselves a superior race—superior to all, including Europeans and Americans. They were very much aware of the racial disdain we had for them. They considered it an insult when we, in conjunction with the British and other European powers, restricted them to a 5-5-3 ratio. That meant they could only build three warships to our five, in perpetuity.

Due to the Exclusion Act by Congress in the 1920s, all Japanese and Asians were excluded from immigration to the United States. The exclusion act also stated that any Japanese already here, even if American born, would not be allowed to own property. The Japanese took notice of this and filed a protest to no avail.

So here we were, racist, bigoted towards anything Japanese, and totally disdainful of them as people. In turn, the Japanese considered us "barbarians," not worthy of any consideration as people. They termed it the "arrogance of the Anglo-Saxon.".

Before you think we are the only racists, consider this: in 1937 the

Panay gunboat (it was in China at the time) was deliberately attacked by the Japanese. They did it to "challenge" the West, and several of our crewmembers were killed.

Incarcerating the Japanese

As I recall, anyone of Japanese background, to us, who had just suffered the attack on our fleet at Pearl Harbor, was "vermin." One has to understand that the Japanese were winning and conquering any and all possessions in the Pacific. Thousands of our men were being rounded up and put into prisoner of war camps without any human consideration whatsoever! We could not imagine the cruelty of the Japanese army towards any American or European prisoners of war. We only heard rumors, but as the war continued, the rumors turned out to be all too true.

As a matter of fact, one of the worries that always came to mind was, "Do not get captured, by all means!"

To illustrate this, one of our flight crews was shot down over the very large base of Rabaul, in the New Guinea area. We later learned that the ones captured were beheaded, all except one, the P.P.C. (Patrol Plane Commander). He was flown to Tokyo for further "intensive" interrogation.

We all knew what that meant.

Our hatred of all Japanese was intense. Thus, when we heard that the Japanese on our West Coast were being incarcerated, we thought it was just, and we heartily approved of this action. We'd been calling the Japanese any number of things, they were basically immediately stripped of their rights and sent into concentration camps. We put entire families into prison and the one thing we forgot, or didn't want to take into consideration, is that they were Americans, just like us. Now that I thoroughly understand what it means to be an American, I am totally ashamed of the incarceration of these Japanese-American citizens.

When the Japanese-American Museum was inaugurated in 1996, I realized that the Japanese-Americans had been victimized. They were truly as American as anybody—I was of Mexican heritage, they were of Japanese. As we know now Japanese-Americans volunteered in great numbers to fight that war. It was their war as well and in fact, they ended up the most decorated part of the American Army that we had at the time. Putting them into prison turned out to be the most un-American thing we could have ever done.

April 30, 1996 I wrote a letter to the Japanese-American National Museum:

April 30, 1996

JAPANESE AMERICAN
NATIONAL MUSEUM
369 East First St.
Los Angeles, CA. 90012

Gentlemen: (Ms. Irene Y. Hirano)

Please accept this heartfelt donation from a man who is still ashamed and guilty for agreeing that this abomination inflicted on fellow Americans in 1942, was the 'American' thing to do!

As you pointed out, and how well I remember the newsreels of the late 1930's, thousands of Americans of German descent, at Madison Square Garden Nazi Rallys, spewing their racial superiority and hatred, and they were never incarcerated "en masse" as were Americans of Japanese back-ground! Such Hypocrisy on our part as Americans!

As an American of Mexican parentage, having grown up in East Los Angeles, having known and gone to school with many Americans of Japanese descent, I should have known better. But young minds are easily influenced by elders and events of the time.

Speaking of 'events of the time,' I am a Pearl Harbor Survivor, a life-time member of the Pearl Harbor Survivors Association, member number 09184L.

With all this in mind, please accept my profound apologies. I am truly sorry!

With Respect,

Peter T. Limon
509 Avenida Adobe,
San Clemente, Ca. 92672
(714) 492 4984

CHAPTER TEN

THE NIGHT I HEARD SAILORS CRY

The night after the attack, a little after 9 p.m., I went up to the gun deck. It was very dark, not only because it was nighttime, but also because of the dark smoke still emitting from the burning battleships.

It was raining and the young men standing gun watch were all under their ponchos—their rain gear. Some were smoking, but no one dared let the light of their cigarette show for fear of getting fired upon. Most were sitting, huddled in groups ready to man the guns.

As I walked by, I heard what I thought was crying, the kind of crying that comes deep from the soul, the heart. I paused to make sure what it was that I was hearing. Yes, it was crying coming from under those ponchos.

It was so involuntary, so uncontrollable. Yes, our sailors were crying unashamedly. It was contagious. I, in turn, could not keep my tears from flowing.

Why did we cry? A stupid question. We cried for our murdered dead, our terrible losses, our wounded pride, our fears and our loneliness.

We cried for how deeply we missed that yesterday, when we had been such a beautiful fighting force. Now we were nothing but broken burning ships. And we cried for our mothers and fathers, our sweethearts and wives, but most of all we cried for our country. The humiliation of it all! How were we ever going to explain this to the country—that we were totally defeated in two hours. How do we explain this to anybody? We were supposed to be the strongest military organization in the world, and we were caught off guard. It kept running through my mind that we were guilty of not being who we were, the guardians of our country. We'd let the country down. The guilt and heartbreak brought on the tears and then more tears. To this day I've wondered if we'd ever be forgiven.

CHAPTER ELEVEN

CONCLUSION

The Japanese, not to mention the Germans, misread the attitude and the pride that is deep in the American psyche, that a murderous insult of this type could not, and would not, go unanswered.

I've often thought to myself, how and why did this war begin? The answer to my question and the reason for this murderous attack without warning was racism. Indeed, racism on both parts, ours and the Japanese. We now see that mutual interaction between nations is the only way to prevent another disaster of this type.

Meanwhile, a half century later, I can only say to those young men who died that day, try to rest well. We now know the answer to that horrible day. It is a day we hope will never be repeated. Thank you from the bottom of my heart for giving your all to our beloved America, and rest well.

Two marine corps dive bomber pilots are being decorated for hits on a Japanese carrier. I am being decorated for participating in the sinking of a Japanese troop ship (that's me in the sailor suit).

Two weeks after the raid on Pearl, we were all allowed to send one telegram home. This is an old copy of what my two sisters received as they waited anxiously for word as to my wellbeing. All the messages were alike; the only difference was the addressee and name of the serviceman. Throughout the nation, families of the servicemen based at Pearl Harbor could only hope and pray that their loved ones were alive and safe. One can only imagine the anxiety of the families and relations not hearing about them for two weeks! My sisters told me it was the worst two weeks of their lives.

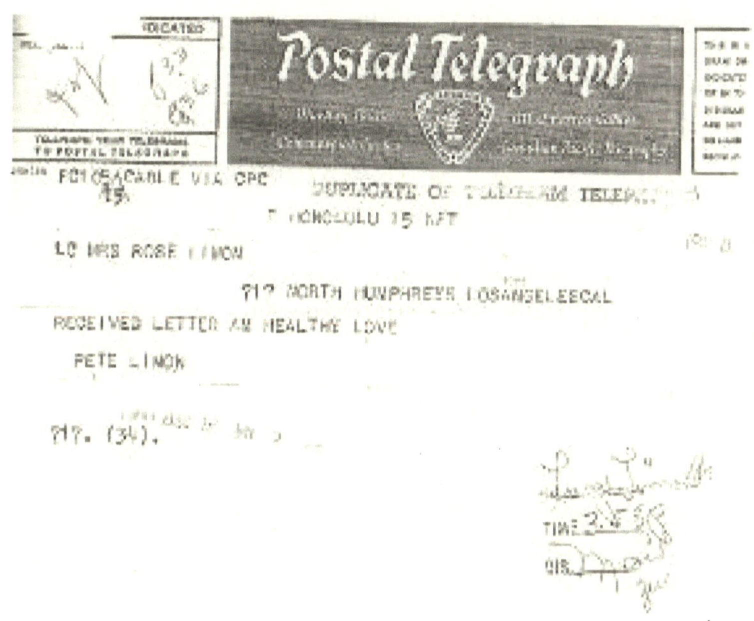

Postal Telegraph

FC1 CABLE VIA CPC

DUPLICATE OF TELEGRAM TELEP...

HONOLULU 15 NFT

LC MRS ROSE LIMON

717 NORTH HUMPHREYS LOSANGELESCAL

RECEIVED LETTER AM HEALTHY LOVE

PETE LIMON

717. (34).

TIME

A Letter From James Forrestal

VP 52 conducted many night attacks against Japanese shipping. We, along with two other PBY squadrons, were awarded the Presidential Unit Citation for the most enemy ships sunk. I personally, along with the other crewmen received the air medal with clusters, denoting many other sinkings of enemy ships. But most important of all to me is a personal letter from Secretary of the Navy James Forrestal, in which he thanked me for my service. The secretary committed suicide after the war. Some say he committed suicide because of the many casualties we suffered at Iwo Jima. He was there and, as senior officer present, he came close to calling off the invasion as so many of our Marines were being killed or wounded. My sadness for him continues to this very day.

THE SECRETARY OF THE NAVY

WASHINGTON

November 27, 1945

My dear Mr. Liman:

I have addressed this letter to reach you after all the formalities of your separation from active service are completed. I have done so because, without formality but as clearly as I know how to say it, I want the Navy's pride in you, which it is my privilege to express, to reach into your civil life and to remain with you always.

You have served in the greatest Navy in the world.

It crushed two enemy fleets at once, receiving their surrenders only four months apart.

It brought our land-based airpower within bombing range of the enemy, and set our ground armies on the beachheads of final victory.

It performed the multitude of tasks necessary to support these military operations.

No other Navy at any time has done so much. For your part in these achievements you deserve to be proud as long as you live. The Nation which you served at a time of crisis will remember you with gratitude.

The best wishes of the Navy go with you into civilian life. Good luck!

Sincerely yours,

James Forrestal

James Forrestal

Mr. Peter Treslavinia Liman
717 N. Humphreys Ave.
Los Angeles, California

www.ingramcontent.com/pod-product-compliance
Lightning Source LLC
LaVergne TN
LVHW090140160826
845673LV00017B/2539

9798751547318